WRITE YOUR OWN

MYSTERY

STORY

by Tish Farrell

First published in the United States in 2006 by
Compass Point Books
A Capstone Imprint
151 Good Counsel Drive
P.O. Box 669
Mankato, MN 56002-0669

Copyright © ticktock Entertainment Ltd 2006
First published in Great Britain in 2006 by ticktock Media Ltd.,
ISBN 1 86007 532 0 PB
A CIP catalogue record for this book is available from the British Library.

This book was manufactured with paper containing at least 10 percent post-consumer waste.

For Compass Point Books
Sue Vander Hook, Nick Healy, Anthony Wacholtz, Nathan Gassman, James Mackey, Abbey Fitzgerald, Catherine Neitge, Keith Griffin, and Carol Jones

For ticktock Entertainment Ltd
Graham Rich, Elaine Wilkinson, John Lingham,
Suzy Kelly, Heather Scott, Jeremy Smith

Library of Congress Cataloging-in-Publication Data
Farrell, Tish.
  Write your own mystery story / by Tish Farrell.
     p. cm. — (Write your own)
  Includes bibliographical references and index.
  Audience: Grade 4-6.
  ISBN 978-0-7565-1641-3 (hardcover)
  ISBN 978-0-7565-1816-5 (paperback)
  1. Detective and mystery stories—Authorship—Juvenile literature. I. Title. II. Series.
  PN3377.5.D4F37 2006
  808.3'872—dc22   2005030730

Visit Compass Point Books on the Internet at *www.capstonepub.com*

Printed in the United States of America in Stevens Point, Wisconsin.
032010
005744R

Get on the case

Do you always figure out "whodunnit" before the book or movie is over? Would you like to create perplexing mysteries of your own? This book will give you the clues and insider tips you need to craft a story that keeps readers guessing. To help you on your way, you will find brainstorming and storytelling exercises that will develop your creative writing skills. Keep in mind, your task as a mystery writer is to uncover a fresh story idea and turn it into a gripping tale that hooks your readers from the first line.

ONTENTS

WANT TO BE A WRITER?

This book is the perfect place to start. It will give you the tools to write your own mystery. Learn how to craft believable characters and perfect plots, along with satisfying beginnings, middles, and endings. Examples from a variety of famous books are used with tips and techniques from published authors to help you on your way.

Get the writing habit

Do timed and regular practice. Real writers make themselves write even when they don't particularly feel like it.

Create a story-writing zone.

Keep a journal.

Keep a notebook—record interesting events and note how people behave and speak.

Generate ideas

Find a character whose story you want to tell. What is his or her problem?

Brainstorm to find out everything about your character.

Research settings, events, and other characters.

Get a mix of good and evil characters.

GETTING STARTED · · · · · · · · · · · SETTING THE SCENE · · · · · · · · · CHARACTERS · · · · · · · · · VIEWPOINT

You can follow your progress by using the bar located on the bottom of each page. The orange color tells you how far along the story-writing process you have gotten. As the blocks are filled out, your story will be growing.

lan

hat is your
ry about?

hat happens?

n the
;inning,
ddle, and end.

ite a synopsis
create story-
rds.

Write

Write the first draft, and then put it aside for a while.

Check spelling and dialogue—does it flow?

Remove unnecessary words.

Does the story have a good end and title?

Avoid clichés.

Publish

Write or print the final draft.

Always keep a copy for yourself.

Send your story to children's magazines, Internet writing sites, competitions, or school magazines.

SES AND PLOTS   WINNING
                       WORDS   HINTS AND TIPS   THE NEXT STEP

When you get to the end of the bar, your book is ready to go! You are an author!
You now need to decide what to do with your book and what your next project should be.
Perhaps it will be a sequel to your story, or maybe something completely different.

BEGIN THE MYSTERY

Unlike real private eyes and police detectives, mystery writers solve their "whodunnits" with a pen and paper in their own homes. They may visit the library or use the Internet to check facts or research an idea, but otherwise they can work in comfort and quiet.

What you need

In addition to pen, paper, books, and the Internet, you may also need to have the following:

- a small notebook that you carry everywhere

- pens with different colored ink

- different colored Post-it notes to mark important book passages or to keep track of ideas

- stick-on stars to highlight your best ideas

- a spiral notebook and scrap paper

- files and folders to keep story ideas safe

- dictionary, thesaurus, and encyclopedia

ur writing place

re you start, you need a special writing place. This
probably be your bedroom, but being a sleuth (a
ctive or investigator), you may like to write where
can watch people—in the park, at school, in a
coffee shop, or at your favorite burger joint. Have
discovering where your best writing place might be.

ttle into a
ory-writing zone

may also need some extra creativity
ers. These could be anything:

usic that helps you think clearly

nagnifying glass, binoculars, and other
s of the investigator's trade

- a hat that you wear only when you're
  writing (Sherlock Holmes had his deerstalker
  hat; you could make a hat or customize one
  you already have)

- puzzles, games, and books on
  code-cracking—anything to exercise
  your powers of deduction

Spend time choosing these things, and make
sure your writing place is special to you.
Special things are going to happen there.

Writer's golden rule

Once you have found your writing place, the
golden rule of becoming a real writer is *Go
there as often as possible and write!*

It really doesn't matter what you write, as long
as you write something.

Writers and investigators have a lot in common: sharp eyes for detail, hunch about things that don't fit, and incurable curiosity. But mystery writers must think u crimes that challenge both their internal sleut and their readers. They must also present it all a believable, exciting story that readers can't put down.

Learn the skills

Learning to become a writer can take a long time. You must train yourself to write regularly, not just when you feel inspired. A brilliant flash of genius might give you a story idea, but only through hard labor will you craft your tale to the final word. Ideally, you should write every day—writing e-mails and journal entries counts. But if you only have an hour free on weekends, make that your writing time. Practice writing just as you would a sport or musical instrument.

Case study

Award-winning writer Kate DiCamillo says that she hates the idea of having to write regularly, but she doesn't let that stop her. Every day, she writes her target of two pages so she feels happy with herself.

Now it's your turn

Brainstorm

Try this brainstorming exercise to unlock your imagination.
Sit quietly in your writing zone for a few moments. Close your
eyes and take four long, deep breaths. Then open your eyes.
Set a stopwatch or timer for two minutes. Write the phrase
"Elementary, my dear Watson" at the top of a piece of paper.
Then write down all the mystery-related words, phrases, and
names that come to your mind. Don't think about them.
Just write things down.

Early success

Great! You've proven you
can write. Give yourself a
gold star. Already you have
found the key to your
imagination. The more you
practice like this, the more
you will develop your
powers of deduction.

TIPS AND TECHNIQUES

*Brainstorming is your most important
writer's tool. Like a set of keys, it
unlocks the "Confidential" files in
your mind and sets your imagination
free. Keep all your brainstorming
notes in a separate file or notebook.
You will need them later.*

Now it's your turn

Set the scene for your mystery

Look over the words or phrases you wrote in the previous exercise. Now imagine that
you've stumbled on some kind of mystery—a crime scene or strange happening. Describe
what you see using five of those words. Even if you don't understand what you have
discovered, try to describe the key details of the scene exactly. Does the discovery frighten
or excite you? What about the sounds, smells, and textures around you? Be specific. You
are recording events that could yield more clues later.

All good writing starts with good reading. There are many different kinds of mystery stories for you to choose from. So what is a mystery story and what makes a good one?

Mysteries seek answers

Great mysteries often begin with a simple question: Who did it? (Or, *whodunnit*, as mystery fans put it.) Characters work to discover the culprit. Along the way, suspense builds as the characters throw themselves into dangerous situations and edge nearer to the truth. Readers can hardly wait to find out what happens next.

Intrigue and entertainment

Mystery stories have puzzles at their heart. The baffling incidents can involve robbery, kidnapping, murder, or disappearance. There might be crimes committed for gain, revenge, or even protection of a loved one. The mystery might be present-day, historical, or futuristic, involving supernatural happenings or international spies.

Sleuths and suspects

The central character usually uses his or her deductive powers to right wrongs and to prove that crime does not pay. Readers also must meet other people in the story. There may be one or more main suspects, and their motives for doing wrong must be believable. They must also have the opportunity and realistic means to carry out their crime.

The mystery and the explanation

After the mystery is revealed, the story goes on to reconstruct the events that explain it. Readers are given clues, which piece together like a jigsaw puzzle to solve the mystery. Cunning writers may use several red herrings (false clues), but the ending must be both satisfying and surprising. Before you start writing, read as many different kinds of mystery stories as possible. They won't all fit this mystery blueprint, but find the ones that intrigue you most. Look at how the writers drop clues. If a good character starts to form in your mind, make notes.

LOG BOOK

Now it's your turn

The hunt is on

Write these words at the top of a new page in your notebook: "The hunt is on." In two minutes, jot down as many different words and phrases you can think of that mean searching and finding (such as detecting, discovering, turning up).

TIPS AND TECHNIQUES

It's good to base your characters on people you know or see—in the mall, on the bus, on the street. Note facial details and odd quirks of behavior.

ES AND PLOTS · · · · · · WINNING WORDS · · · · · · SCINTILLATING SPEECH · · · · · · HINTS AND TIPS · · · · · · THE NEXT STEP · · · · · ·

11

Great writers will help you find your own writer's "voice." Read with your writer's mind switched on. Of course, you want to enjoy a story. First, read it for pleasure, but then go back to it. Study it. Do the characters convince you? Does the plot work? Do you like the ending? Where are the clues cleverly laid? How does the writer create tension and suspense?

Find your writer's voice

Once you start reading as a writer, you will notice that each story has its own rhythm and range of language that stays the same throughout the book. You will get to know different writers' styles. Richard Peck writes nothing like Edgar Allan Poe. Anthony Horowitz is worlds apart from Arthur Conan Doyle. In other words, you will discover that every writer has a distinctive voice—one that your mystery-solving mind will soon recognize.

Now it's your turn

Find your voice

Pick an exciting scene from your favorite mystery book. Rewrite it as if you were there. Give yourself a leading role—either as sleuth or criminal.

Experiment

Once you've found a writer whose books you really enjoy, it' tempting to stick with that writer. Don't do that. You'll proba end up imitating the way he or she writes. Experiment with your reading. Reading a historical novel might give you some interesting background details for your mystery story.

WRITERS' VOICES

Look at the kinds of words these authors use. Do they use lots of adjectives? What about the length of their sentences? Which style do you prefer to read?

ARTHUR CONAN DOYLE

I had called upon my friend Sherlock Holmes. ... He was lounging upon the sofa. ... A lens and a forceps lying upon the seat of the chair suggested that the hat had been suspended in this manner for the purpose of examination.

Arthur Conan Doyle, *The Adventure of the Blue Carbuncle*

CAROLYN KEENE

"Talk about sleazy. Look at this headline," Bess Marvin said indignantly, sliding Today's Times *across the kitchen table to Nancy.*

"The poor guy's dead, and all anyone can talk about is his money."

Carolyn Keene, *Make No Mistake* (Nancy Drew)

ANTHONY HOROWITZ

Alex looked up and realized that everyone was staring at him. Mr. Donovan had just asked him something. He quickly scanned the blackboard, taking in the figures. "Yes, sir," he said, "x equals seven and y is fifteen."

The math teacher sighed. "Yes, Alex. You're absolutely right. But actually I was just asking you to open the window."

Anthony Horowitz, *Stormbreaker*

EDGAR ALLAN POE

During the whole of a dull, dark, and soundless day in the autumn of the year, when the clouds hung oppressively low in the heavens, I had been passing alone, on horseback, through the singularly dreary tract of country, and at length found myself, as the shades of evening drew on, within the view of the melancholy House of Usher.

Edgar Allan Poe, *The Fall of the House of Usher*

If you ask writers where they get their story ideas, they will probably answer, "Everywhere." Finding a good mystery story depends on how you look at things. If you think your life is boring and unexciting, then you'll find it hard. But if you look at your world with undercover eyes, plenty of stories will crop up.

Hunt for the story

A mystery story is a puzzle—something unusual that doesn't fit, something unexplained, illegal, or spooky. It could be happening right next door. Imagine you are a private eye waiting for a key suspect to show up at a house on your street. From where will you watch? Or maybe you have seen an odd message in the lost-and-found column of the local paper. Who's it for? Who might respond?

Insider info

To be a writer, you must search inside your own head for ideas. Break into those "Confidential" files that you have tucked away in your subconscious mind—all the stories you've ever read, the TV shows you've watched, and all the facts you've ever learned. Brainstorming and scribbling down your first thoughts is one way to start accessing all that story-making material.

Focus the mind

If you have binoculars, use them to look down your street. Or sit in a shopping mall and watch an area that is buzzing with activity. For 15 minutes, log everything that happens there. Describe how people behave. That boy on the bench checking his watch: Is he looking for his friend, or is there something more sinister going on? Take notes on his appearance—he could be a suspect. All the details you record could lead to a story. You are learning a mystery writer's most essential skill—studying people and their behaviors. Ask questions. What if the boy's dad is robbing a bank, and the boy is the lookout? As soon as you ask questions, your imagination will start producing ideas.

TIPS AND TECHNIQUES

A story idea is only the start. Making it into a good story takes hard work and lots of thinking. Brainstorm when you are bored or nervous. Make lists. How many different ways can you describe how you're feeling? Are you bored as concrete? Quivery as a rat's tail?

Now it's your turn

What's the mystery?

In all good stories, the hero has a personal problem. In a mystery story, the problem and the mystery might be the same thing. Story problems begin with writers asking questions such as, "What if my dad turned out to be a bank robber?" Use this idea now, and take 20 minutes to rewrite your own history. Ask yourself questions: How did I discover my dad was a bank robber? How does it make me feel? What am I going to do about it? Be tragic or comic, but pour out your feelings. If you think you have the makings of a good story, take time to develop it.

BUILD A CASE

One sure-fire way to develop mystery story ideas is to study your local newspaper. Start a scrapbook collection of good stories: robberies, missing people, scandals over land development. Again, pose questions as you scan the paper. Highlight any interviews with real people in which they express their views or feelings. All this will help you create your own characters.

Research

Your local library probably has old newspapers on microfilm. Perhaps there was some big crime story in the past that the librarian can help you track down. Or maybe there is a local mystery—an eerie house or the unexplained disappearance of a wealthy individual.

If you look around, you will find that the world is full of puzzling stories. Read fiction and nonfiction. Search the Internet for ideas. Of course, you can even get lots of valuable information from all those TV detective shows.

Now it's your turn

Your dad is a bank robber

Try building on the last writing exercise (from page 15), in which you imagined your father as a bank robber. You will need all kinds of human details to make a believable story. You'll also need some technical information about break-ins. The criminology section in your library may have a book on famous bank robberies. Or perhaps your fictional father devised a computer program that did the job instead. In that case, computer fraud is the topic to research.

16

GETTING STARTED · SETTING THE SCENE · · · · · · · · · · · · · CHARACTERS · · · · · · · · · VIEWPOINT

Case study

"Elementary, my dear Watson!"
Sir Arthur Conan Doyle was a doctor by
profession. He trained at Edinburgh
University in Scotland, where he was
influenced a great deal by Professor John
Bell, who used deductive reasoning to
diagnose disease. Doyle was so impressed
by Bell's
methods that
he applied
the same
principles
when he
created
Sherlock
Holmes.

TIPS AND TECHNIQUES

Use your own technical knowledge for story
ideas.If you have special skills or interests, then think
how you can use your specialist knowledge. Have you
read something about microchips or miniature listening
devices? Does someone in your family work in a place
that has plenty of intrigue? These insights are real gifts for
a writer. Use them for all they are worth. When watching
a TV mystery, don't forget to make notes on any useful
technical information.

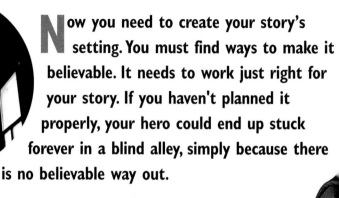

Now you need to create your story's setting. You must find ways to make it believable. It needs to work just right for your story. If you haven't planned it properly, your hero could end up stuck forever in a blind alley, simply because there is no believable way out.

Drop hints

If particular places or things are going to be crucial to solving the mystery, their existence must be established early on in the story. They must be part of the landscape that the reader can picture, though not in an obvious way.

Suppose a large marble urn in an old lady's house is a possible murder weapon. Early on, the reader needs to see it—but not consider it important. One way to do this is to mention it in the middle of other things, something like this:

"What an eerie place! I stepped through the door and a grizzly attacked me—all teeth and claws. It took me a moment to realize he was stuffed, but by then I'd swung around into a huge urn, which teetered on its stand. I steadied it just as it was about to fall on me. All around on the walls, grim antique faces sneered down."

Later, when a victim is found apparently crushed by the urn, readers will think they know exactly what happened. But was it an accident, or was it only made to look like one? Or will it turn out to be a red herring?

Now it's your turn

See it from a different viewpoint

Go back to your brainstormed notes from page 9. Can you see your setting more clearly now? So far, you have probably looked at it from the viewpoint of your hero. Now, learn more about the place by writing from a different viewpoint. For example, if it's where a robbery has been committed, describe it from the thief's point of view, as he cases the joint in advance, planning how he will carry out the crime.

Build your story's landscape

Create a setting by starting at a specific place and building the landscape around it. Or work from a general landscape and zoom in on a specific location later. You could draw a map of the area and use colored stickers to highlight the location of each crime. Think how your local streets, parks, stores, and landmarks might serve your story.

Now it's your turn

Be a real detective

It's time to do some legwork. Study places that are like the ones you want to use in your story. You could start with your own bedroom. Then go to your school, a museum, train station, or park. Take a notebook. Imagine you're seeing the place for the first time. What do you notice? A particular smell or atmosphere? Certain noises or textures? Do a two-minute brainstorm, noting five things you see, hear, feel, and smell.

TIPS AND TECHNIQUES

If you want to have a historical setting for your mystery, make sure you know your facts. Read up at the library before you start writing your own story.

PAINT THE PICTURE

Both new and experienced writers can fall into the trap of writing too much description. If it gets in the way of the story, readers will either skip it or close the book. The trick is to say just enough for readers to place your characters in the scene.

Set the scene: Recipe #1

If your hero or hero's assistant is the narrator, then this character's voice will also help to capture the reader's interest. Frances O'Roark Dowell's murder mystery, *Dovey Coe*, is set in rural North Carolina. It is told from prime suspect Dovey's first-person viewpoint. In the following excerpt, the description of setting is used to tell us several things about Dovey. See how many separate pieces of information about Dovey are stated or implied.

Every time I start complaining about having to walk a half mile down the mountain to school, I remember how lucky we are to own our land. It ain't much—four acres, a five-room house, and a barn—but it keeps us Coes from being beholden to Homer Caraway, and I'd walk ten miles to school to keep it that way.

Frances O'Roark Dowell, *Dovey Coe*

Recipe #2

Scene setting can be used to create mood, mystery, and suspense in the first lines of the book. In *Big Mouth & Ugly Girl*, Joyce Carol Oates' setting is stark and ordinary, but she immediately introduces mystery and hooks our curiosity:

It was an ordinary January afternoon, a Thursday, when they came for Matt Donaghy. They came for him in fifth period, which was Matt's study period, in room 220 of Rocky High School, Westchester County.

Joyce Carol Oates, *Big Mouth & Ugly Girl*

Recipe #3

There will be times in your story for straightforward scene setting. Author Enid Blyton excelled at this. In *Five on a Treasure Island*, she sums up Julian, Dick, and Anne's first impression of their cousin's house in two sentences:

> *They liked it. It felt old and rather mysterious somehow, and the furniture was old and very beautiful.*
> Enid Blyton, *Five on a Treasure Island*

Recipe #4

Find ways to trigger your readers' senses to make a scene more real. At the start of Charlie Higson's *SilverFin*, a boy is preparing to sneak under a barbed-wire fence to poach fish from an estate. Extra tension is added when readers know the boy will have to cross open ground. Notice, too, that specific plant names are given to make us picture the place and believe the story:

> *The afternoon light was fading into evening, taking all the detail from the land with it. Here, on this side of the fence, among the thick gorse and juniper and low rowan trees, he was well hidden, but soon ... soon he was going under the wire, and on the other side the tree cover quickly fell away.*
> Charlie Higson, *SilverFin*

Now it's your turn

Describe your hero

Choose things that reflect your hero's character, interests, and tastes. What's under your hero's pillow? Where does he or she hide things? What kinds of clothes are in the closet? Once you have considered this, you should be able to picture your hero more clearly.

DISCOVER YOUR HERO

Whether you have one hero (protagonist) or more, that character or group must be the center of the story and will ultimately solve the mystery. You must care about your heroes as if they were friends and find ways to make readers care about them. Avoid making them perfect—perfect people are dull.

Heroic qualities

Imagine meeting your hero. You like something about this person right away, and you want to be friends. What do you especially admire? Find out as much as possible before you start. Is there something in your hero's past that sets the mystery in motion?

Inspiration from others

You can base a hero on a classic detective, but don't simply copy someone. That would be plagiarism. Take some characteristics, adapt them, and mix them with real people or other characters. For example, if you mixed a bit of Sherlock Holmes with an ace student, you might end up with a character like Hermione in the Harry Potter books.

TIPS AND TECHNIQUES

Try searching through the phone book if you can't think of a good name for your hero.

Describe your investigator near the start of your story. Otherwise, readers might imagine someone being tall and dark, and you later reveal her to be red-haired and small. You'll risk losing a reader's attention in the confusion.

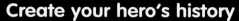

Create your hero's history

Make your hero's history brief, but make sure you remember what it is as you write the story.

Give your hero flaws

In *Dovey Coe*, Dovey is so likable, it is hard to understand how she has been charged with murder. However, she does speak her mind, often in scathing terms. She also sets out to make a very public enemy of Parnell Caraway. "I'd just as soon shoot him as look at him," she says at one point. Later, this is used as evidence. But she tells us, "I admit that's my biggest drawback, not thinking things through far enough."

Now it's your turn

On the record

Open a file on your hero. Make out an official report that you can add to later as more ideas come to you. Begin by filling out the personal details: name, age, address, nationality, previous addresses, and details of immediate relatives. Describe your hero's appearance. Give details of how the character lives and what he or she does. Do some sketches, too, or cut out faces from magazines and newspapers.

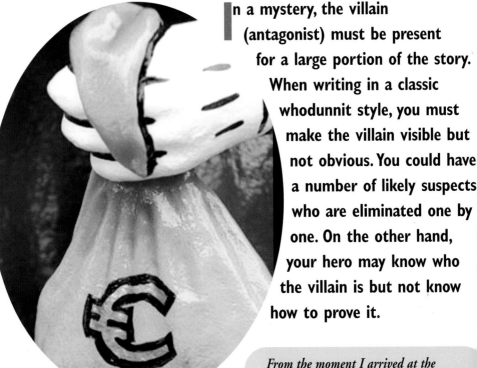

In a mystery, the villain (antagonist) must be present for a large portion of the story. When writing in a classic whodunnit style, you must make the villain visible but not obvious. You could have a number of likely suspects who are eliminated one by one. On the other hand, your hero may know who the villain is but not know how to prove it.

Motivation

Before you start writing, find out what makes your villain bad. Is he or she a bully or someone who is hungry for power? Does your villain want money or revenge? Is he or she a victim of circumstance or just plain evil? Here, Herod Sayle explains his motivation in *Stormbreaker*:

From the moment I arrived at the school, I was mocked and bullied. Because of my size. Because of the color of my skin. Because I couldn't speak English well. Because I wasn't one of them. They had names for me. Herod Smell. Goat-boy. The Dwarf. They played tricks on me. … My trousers ripped off me and hung out on the flagpole.

Anthony Horowitz, *Stormbreaker*

Case study

Legendary mystery writer Agatha Christie said she "discovered" the murderer in her first detective story while she was in Torquay in southern England. She saw a dark, bearded man who was the mysterious-looking character she needed to get her story going.

Villainous profiles

Creating a good villain can make a fantasy story so much more exciting. Here are some ideas for different types of villains:

AN OBVIOUS VILLAIN

Dr. Watson describes Dr. Grimesby Roylott as he bursts into Sherlock Holmes' home. It's a ...ting description for a most devious killer.

> A large face, seared with a thousand wrinkles, burned yellow with every passion ... while his deepset, bile-shot eyes, and his high thin, fleshless nose, gave him the resemblance to a fierce old bird of prey.
>
> Arthur Conan Doyle,
> *The Adventure of the Blue Carbuncle*

MASTER CRIMINAL

...*Stormbreaker*, Anthony Horowitz' ...ain, Herod Sayle, is a terrorist. He wants ...ake revenge on the prime minister and ...schoolchildren in general because he ...so tormented and bullied at school.

AN UNUSUAL VILLAIN

In *Wolf* by Gillian Cross, the villain is a terrorist and someone unexpected, too, but for much of the story we share the main character's fearful sense of being stalked by an unknown terror.

TRADING PLACES

In *Dovey Coe*, there's another kind of twist. We know in the first few lines that Parnell has been killed, and Dovey has been charged with his murder. But the victim is the villain, and the hero is the only suspect.

AN UNEXPECTED VILLAIN

In Zizou Corder's *Lionboy*, Rafi Sadler is the young man who kidnaps Charlie Ashanti's scientist parents and tries to kidnap Charlie, too. He is known to all of them as a neighbor. Charlie even admires him a little.

TIPS AND TECHNIQUES

If you don't know what your villain looks like, do some people-watching. Take out your notebook. Play "20 Questions" with your villain. Ask 20 different things about his or her appearance and history. See how much you can figure out.

Your sleuth will need people to discuss the case with or to interact with in other ways, so you need some supporting characters. Scenes with minor characters are the best way to show the reader what your heroes are really like. You can show them being ingenious or sometimes being too clever and jumping to the wrong conclusion.

The most famous of them all

In Sherlock Holmes stories, Dr. Watson is both assistant and narrator. This is a useful device. Dr. Watson is often slow and describes events at his own pace, not revealing Holmes' solution until the end. In this way, he builds suspense. If we knew things as soon as Holmes did, there would be less excitement and surprise.

Build relationships

The main characters in mysteries are often lonely or isolated in some way. But in *Dovey Coe*, the heroine, Dovey, is part of a loving family. This gives her a possible motive for killing Parnell—he wants to marry her sister Caroline, and he makes dark threats about sending their deaf brother, Amos, to an institution.

TIPS AND TECHNIQUES

Supporting characters (even animals) must add to the story in some way. If they don't have a job to do, cut them out. The conversations between helpers and heroes add variety and interest and are a good way to reveal the thought processes involved in solving the mystery.

GETTING STARTED — SETTING THE SCENE — CHARACTERS — VIEWPOINT

Now it's your turn

Write biographies

Choose five people whom you feel you know very well. They could be friends of the family or classmates. Write a brief biography of each one. Make the person as fascinating as possible in no more than three sentences.

Use quick fixes

Supporting characters—helpers or suspects—will not be as fully developed as your hero, so you must find ways to plant them in readers' minds. Be quick and interesting so they add to the story, not hold it up. Here we meet Herod Sayle's trusty assistant, Mr. Grin, for the first time in *Stormbreaker*. We won't forget him easily, and we assume he means trouble.

> *From a distance it looked as if he was smiling, but as he grew closer Alex gasped. The man had two horrendous scars, one on each side of his mouth, twisting all the way up to his ears. It was as if someone had attempted to cut his face in half.*
> Anthony Horowitz, *Stormbreaker*

Surprising sidekicks

Your detectives may not always be human. In Walter R. Brooks' *Freddy the Detective*, the main character is a mystery-loving pig.

CHOOSE A POINT OF VIEW

Before you can write your opening line, you must decide who is telling your story. Do you want to tell the readers everything that is happening—show all the different characters and how they are behaving or feeling? Or do you want to tell one particular person's story (such as your hero)? Will the hero or another character tell the story?

Decide on your point of view

First-person viewpoint

In detective stories, events are often described in the first-person point of view. This instantly makes everything sound more believable, but it can only give that one person's observations. Sherlock Holmes' cases are all related by Dr. Watson. This is how Watson starts his account of "Th Adventure of the Speckled Band":

> *On glancing over my notes of the seventy-odd cases in which I have during the last eight years studied the methods of my friend Sherlock Holmes, I find many tragic, some comic, a large number merely strange, but none commonplace.*
> Arthur Conan Doyle, "The Adventure of the Speckled Band"

Omniscient viewpoint

Nancy Drew stories are told from the all-seeing—omniscient—point of view. This is also called th objective view. You are not siding with one character or another. You can describe everything, but is less personal or involving than other viewpoints.

> *Matt whirled round to face Nancy. "What are you doing here?" he asked. Ignoring Matt, Nancy said to Jake Loomis, "Let Bess go." Bess' eyes were wide with fear, and she was trembling. Her arm was twisted painfully behind her, but Loomis didn't release his grip.*
> Carolyn Keene, *Nancy Drew: Make No Mistake*

d-person viewpoint

third-person point of view tells the story by following one character
explaining his or her thoughts and feelings. The author
reveal other characters' thoughts or feelings except
ugh dialogue. The viewpoint character can guess
observation but might not get it right. The
point character can't talk about things he or she
't seen, unless another character has given him
er the information. For example:

> *If only they could all be there together on
> e steps for an hour or so. Meg knew she'd feel
> tter. There was so much that needed telling.*
> tty Ren Wright, *A Ghost in the Window*

iple third-person viewpoint

ort stories, it is usual to stick to one
acter's point of view, but novels sometimes
several or multiple third-person viewpoints.
g several viewpoints can add drama. One
acter's view of events might be very different
another's. You can also choose to switch
points at the moment of a cliffhanger—when
ething dangerous or exciting is about to happen.

Now it's your turn

Change views

Write a short scene. Your hero is pursuing the villain. First
write from the all-seeing viewpoint. Describe the behavior of
both characters. Then rewrite it in the third person, giving
only your hero's viewpoint of the pursuit. Finally, write in
the first person, as if you are the hero. Read your efforts aloud
to yourself. Which one do you prefer and why?

TELL YOUR STORY'S STORY

When your story starts simmering in your mind, it's a good idea to write a brief accou of it. Write down what you would say if someone asked you, "What's it about?" This is called a synopsis. A good synopsis will get others to read your work. But don't give away the ending.

Visit a library or bookstore to look at as many mystery books as you can. Read the blurbs—the publishers' information on the back. See how each one says just enough to make you want to read the book. The back cover of *The Ruby in the Smoke*, by Philip Pullman, captures the reader's interest from the first sentence:

> "Sally Lockhart is sixteen, an orphan, and she's just struck a man dead. Not with a weapon, though she has a pistol, and probably the heart to use it. Sally killed Mr. Higgs with just three words—the Seven Blessings. Unfortunately, she still has no idea what they mean, and why her drowned father's colleague dies of fear when he heard them."

The blurb for Terence Blacker's *The Angel Factory* conjures up a more mysterious scenario that invites the reader to pick up the book and find out more:

> "For Thomas Wisdom, life is perfect—caring parents, nice house, loads of friends. Even his dog is just great. But Thomas senses that something at home is wrong. With the help of his friend Gip, he hacks into his father's computer. What he discovers there takes him on a journey into the unimaginable—to a place they call the Angel Factory."

Write your blurb

Sum up your own story in a single striking sentence—two at most. Then introduce the hero and outline the main action in no more than three short paragraphs. Don't give away the ending.

Make a story map

Now you have a synopsis that says what your story is about. You have a cast of characters and a setting, and you know from whose viewpoint you wish to tell the tale. The last thing you need before you start is a story map.

Plan your story into scenes

Before filmmakers can start filming, they must know the main story episodes and decide how they can best tell their story in filmed images. To help them, they map out the plot (the sequence of events) in a series of sketches called storyboards. You can do this for your story. Draw the main episodes in pictures. Add a few notes that say what is happening in each scene.

Think about your theme

At the same time, you might think about your story's theme. What is the central idea? This will shape your villain's motives for committing the crime, but it will only be revealed in your hero's final solution to the mystery.

TIPS AND TECHNIQUES

If you're writing a synopsis and find a flaw in your story, then rethink the plan for your story. Don't try to write it with the hope that no one else will notice the problem. They will.

Create a synopsis

Before they start writing, authors often list all their chapters or scenes and briefly write down what will happen in each one. T[his] is called a chapter synopsis. It provides the mystery writer wit[h] skeleton plot, which helps to keep their story on track.

A famous example

Here is the skeleton of the plot in the Sherlock Holmes stor[y] "The Adventure of the Speckled Band":

1. Helen Stoner arrives at Holmes' place, saying she's afraid for her life.
2. She tells Holmes about the mysterious death of her t[win] sister and her dying words abou[t] speckled band.
3. She gives some family histo[ry] and tells of her violent stepfat[her] Dr. Roylett, who controls the money her mother left her.
4. After she leaves, Dr. Roylett burs[ts] in and threatens Holmes if he starts [to] interfere.
5. Holmes and Watson travel to Stok[e] Moran, Roylett's home, to investig[ate] they discover several strange feature[s] the dead sister's room.
6. Later they go secretly to spend the nig[ht] in the room, and Holmes warns Watson [of] the grave danger.
7. In the night, Holmes sounds the alar[m] lashing out with his cane.
8. A scream comes from Dr. Roylett's room. They find him dead with a speckled band around his head.
9. Holmes explains the case to Watson.

TIPS AND TECHNIQUES

Don't let a novel's length put you off from starting one. If you use the story map approach, it may be no more difficult to write a novel than it is to write a finely tuned short story.

Novels versus short stories

Novels have beginnings, middles, and ends, just like short stories, but novels are more complex. They have more details, more character development, and (probably) several subplots. The chapters make the storytelling manageable. Each chapter has a beginning, middle, and end, but it also carries the story forward, adding more mystery and creating more suspense.

Expand a short story

"The Adventure of the Speckled Band" is a short story. But once you have worked out the main scenes, you could develop each one into a separate chapter and create a novel. To turn "The Adventure of the Speckled Band" into a novel, look at each scene summary and think how to make it into an episode that shows readers more about the characters and their problems. Chapter 1 could start with Helen Stoner waking in terror and then

going to London to seek help. You could show all the difficulties she has leaving the house secretly. A novel, then, is not a short story made longer, but a short story made deeper. The suspense is built up from chapter to chapter, and any mysteries are spun out so that readers are drawn more deeply into the story.

Now it's your turn

Weave a story web

If you're still struggling to come up with a plot for your mystery, get a large piece of paper. In the center, draw a circle. Inside the circle, draw a rough sketch of your hero. As you are drawing, imagine that you are that hero, looking outside the circle, trying to solve a riddle. Then draw six spokes from your hero circle. Each spoke leads to an empty circle. In one minute, without thinking deeply, write one thing in each circle. It can be an object or a piece of information—the dog didn't bark, all the doors and windows were locked at the crime scene, a torn-up plane ticket. The wilder your thoughts, the more likely they will lead to something you can use.

Mystery stories should begin with a mystery. An intriguing first sentence is a good start. Readers must know at once that there will be unusual riddles to solve. But a mystery story is also about people, and the heroes will have their own problems, or at least some pressing reason to solve the mystery.

Hook your readers

At the start of your story, bait your hook with the tastiest tidbits, so the reader will bite. But you also must lay solid foundations so that as you build your story, you wil end up with something strong. Therefore, it is essential that you know your mystery story's ending before you start writing. Then you can work backward, dropping hints and clues in advance. This is called foreshadowing, an important storytelling tool.

Case study

Writer Wilkie Collins (right) said this about how to treat readers: "Make 'em laugh, make 'em cry, make 'em wait."

Now it's your turn

Good beginnings

Write the opening scene of your story. Introduce the hero and the mystery. If possible, include some action. Look at ways to hook the reader's interest and curiosity. Or be spooky. Decide if there's any important information that needs to be slipped in at this point. When you have finished, go back and concentrate on your first sentence. Is it as exciting as you can make it?

Good starts

For a good beginning, create suspense, make the hero engaging, and set the tone. It may be dramatic, spooky, humorous, or chilling. Here are two examples:

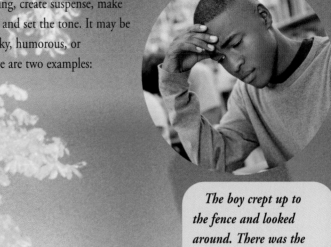

My name is ovey Coe, and I ckon it don't atter if you like me not. I'm here to y the record raight, to let you ow them folks ying I done rrible things are ars. I aim to prove too. I hated arnell Caraway as uch as the next rson, but I didn't ll him.

ances O'Roark owell, *Dovey Coe*

The boy crept up to the fence and looked around. There was the familiar sign …
KEEP OUT!
PRIVATE PROPERTY.
TRESPASSERS WILL BE SHOT.
And hanging next to it, just to make sure that the message was clearly understood, were the bodies of several dead animals. Strung up like criminals, wire twisted round their broken necks.

Charlie Higson, *SilverFin*

TIPS AND TECHNIQUES

learn how to write smack-in-the-eye first sentences, go to the library and read as many as ossible. Make a note of your favorites. Story beginnings introduce the mystery, the hero, and e start of the quest.

BUILD SUSPENSE

Once your investigator is hot on the trail of mystery solving, think about building up the excitement bit by bit, until you reach the climax of your story. Don't put your most thrilling action in the opening scenes. Save the best until last.

Investigate the suspects

In most criminal investigations, there are likely to be several suspects. Intrigue your readers by building a good case against each one. This will require all your mystery writer's cunning. Both investigator and readers must believe that every suspect is a real possibility—or at least until some new clue gives them a watertight alibi.

Throw in more complications

Send your hero off on a quest and then make things really tough. For example, in Zizou Corder's *Lionboy*, the hero, Charlie, stows away on a circus ship to find his kidnapped parents. The chase is hard enough, but once onboard, he agrees to rescue some lions from their cruel trainer. Now he has to dodge his pursuers and reach Venice, all with six lions depending on him.

False endings

Your case is cracked. The prime suspect is in jail. But just as your hero is set to close the casebook, another crime is committed—the same pattern as before, but it is much more evil or shocking. Now it's time to track down the real culprit, but can your hero measure up this time?

Maintain the action

Plenty of action will keep readers reading, but don't include chases or fights just for the sake of it. Action scenes should arise naturally from your characters' own plans. Use them to show readers new things about your characters. Keep them sharp and to the point.

Time is running out

If your sleuth is time-challenged, you instantly add drama. Perhaps he or she must find evidence to clear a client before a court case closes. Maybe your hero must track down the real culprit, who is about to flee the country or commit another crime.

Now it's your turn

Include flaws and weaknesses

A hero's flaws and weaknesses can add complications to a mystery story. For example, a vivid imagination might cause your hero to jump to the wrong conclusions. A grudge might make him or her think old enemies are guilty, when they aren't. In five minutes, brainstorm your first thoughts about weaknesses of the hero in your story. How can your hero's faults make the tale more exciting?

TIPS AND TECHNIQUES

To make the middle of your story gripping, add complications and twists. Pile on the challenges. Lay false trails. Make your sleuth have hard times.

SES AND PLOTS · · · · · | WINNING · · · · · · | · SCINTILLATING SPEECH · · · · · · | · HINTS AND TIPS · · · · · · | · THE NEXT STEP · · · · · · · · · · ·
WORDS

37

Finding a good ending is the hardest part of writing a mystery. As the writer, you will know "whodunnit" right from the start. You will also have worked hard to lay all the necessary clues as the story unfolds. But when the final piece of the jigsaw puzzle is put in place, readers must be both surprised at your solution and satisfied that you haven't cheated them.

Tie up loose ends

All the trails of your story's middle must now come to an exciting climax. The conflicts must be resolved without loose ends, and your hero must have learned something or changed in some way. Mystery story endings are usually concerned with wrongs being righted. Some have a final cunning twist; others end with some dry humor. Most endings aim to be hopeful rather than completely happy.

Use humor

Sherlock Holmes often has a wry comment to make as he concludes his investigations. In "The Adventure of the Speckled Band," the wicked Dr. Grimesby Roylett meets a just end after murdering one stepdaughter and attempting to murder a second. Holmes foils the

murder. Roylett is killed by the venomous snake that he has trained to crawl down a bell-pull into his stepdaughter's bedroom. At the end, Holmes admits to Watson that the blows of his cane drove the reptile back to attack its owner.

> *In this way I am no doubt indirectly responsible for Dr. Grimesby Roylett's death, and I cannot say that it is likely to weigh very heavily upon my conscience.*
>
> Arthur Conan Doyle,
> "The Adventure of the
> Speckled Band"

...dings that suggest a new beginning

...od endings often refer in some way to the beginning of the story. This will remind readers where ...tale started and make the point that something important has changed. At the start of Avi's *Who ...e the Wizard of Oz*, Toby and his twin sister, Becky, have to solve a mystery at the library, where ...e rare books have been stolen. They uncover the secret of a woman who hates children's books ...the treasure she wants for herself. The twins have to work together to find the treasure before ...does. At the end of the story, Toby says, "A good children's book is a book of promises. And ...mises are to keep … and share."

TIPS AND TECHNIQUES

Study TV mysteries such as The X-Files and even Scooby-Doo. Think about the patterns of these stories—their beginnings, middles, and endings. Do all good mysteries have certain things in common? Watch carefully. Take notes.

...d endings are ones that:

...ick readers by springing a totally surprising solution

...il to show how the characters have changed in some way

...e too grim and leave the reader with no hope

...zzle out

Now it's your turn

Choose your own ending

Can you think of another ending to your favorite mystery story? Could someone else have committed the crime? If so, why not write it? Go back and read both versions later to see which you prefer. Use your own ending to write another story.

MAKE YOUR WORDS WORK

Writing with bite means sticking to the point and using words wisely. The scene should be set as quickly as possible. You must choose the most striking details. Mix them with action, and trigger the senses to keep your readers hooked.

Economy of words

Here is the opening setting from Leon Garfield's historical ghost and murder mystery, *The Empty Sleeve*. Notice the strong first sentence hook. His description of the weather sets the tone:

> *It takes all sorts to make a world, but only one to unmake it. On a well-remembered Saturday morning in January, when the air was murderous with wind and snow, like a madman made of feathers, a solitary old man trudged along a street in Rotherhithe, battered, blinded and bewildered by the weather.*
> Leon Garfield, *The Empty Sleeve*

Is there a single word in the Leon Garfield excerpt that you would like to leave out? Probably not. Read your own work aloud. You will likely hear where you have written rambling sentences with too many unnecessary words.

Use words to build images

Another way to quickly bring scenes alive is to use imagery. In *Hoot*, author Carl Hiaason uses a simile to help describe a boy running along a sidewalk. "The soles of his bare feet looked as black as barbecue coals," Hiaason writes. A simile is when you say something is like something else.

TIPS AND TECHNIQUES

A metaphor is when you say a man is a fox, meaning that he's dishonest; a simile is when you say he moves like a fox, meaning he is quick.

| GETTING STARTED | SETTING THE SCENE | CHARACTERS | VIEWPOINT |

Vary the mood

If a story stays in the same mood from start to finish, it's going to lose readers. Author Anthony Horowitz is great at orchestrating suspense—building to climaxes with wild action. Then he gives readers some light relief with quieter moments that are a welcome break from the drama.

Change the rhythm

Changing the rhythm and length of your sentences is another way to keep readers reading. Action scenes should focus on what is happening. But if you are building up for something scary, spin out longer phrases, adding pauses and detail that make the scene more real. Imagine yourself sneaking up on your reader. Build the tension, and then strike.

Now it's your turn

Try some word plays

Cut up scrap paper into at least 60 small squares. Brainstorm 30 adjectives and 30 nouns, or use a dictionary, thesaurus, or other reference book and pick them out at random. Write one word on each square. Keep the nouns and adjectives separate. Then keep dealing yourself one from each pile. See what pairs you get.

TALL   monstrosity

TREE   ingenious

WALLS   famished

USE DRAMATIC DIALOGUE

Dialogue plays a big part in many mystery stories. In the Nancy Drew and Hardy Boys books, dialogue often carries the plot. For example, a lot of puzzling over clues is reported in conversations between the Hardy Boys and other characters. Dialogue must flow smoothly and sound just right.

Listen in

The best way to learn about dialogue is to switch on your listening ear and eavesdrop. Tune in to people's conversations. Pay attention to rhythm and turns of phrase. Watch people's body language when they are whispering or arguing. Remember, all the great investigators pay close attention to human behavior and are naturally nosy.

Look, listen, and absorb.

Now it's your turn

Discuss the evidence

Study the dialogue in a Nancy Drew or Hardy Boys book. Write a short scene in your own story where your sleuth is discussing something with a friend or assistant. Show them talking about "the evidence"—do they disagree or come up with solutions? What do they decide to do next?

re's some dialogue from a Nancy Drew book:

> *"Where do we start?" George asked.*
>
> *"Well, I'd like to check out Gary Page's credentials at the Chicago Clarion," Nancy suggested.*
>
> *George looked at her watch. "If we leave right now, we could be back by early evening."*
>
> *"Well, I already believe Matt," Bess said. "But if it'll make you guys feel better, let's go."*
>
> *Nancy frowned. "I wish I had a photo of him to take with us, to show to the people at the paper."*
>
> *"No problem," said Bess, blushing a little. "I just happen to have a very recent picture of him." She fumbled in her purse and drew out an instant photo of Matt.*
>
> *"Where did you get that?" Nancy and George asked at the same time.*
>
> Carolyn Keene, *Make No Mistake* (Nancy Drew)

fiction, if a speaker stumbles, it is only suggested with occasional stammered rds. Dialogue doesn't copy natural speech. It gives an edited pression of how people speak.

llow convention

tten dialogue follows certain ventions or rules. It is usual to t a new paragraph with every speaker. What they say is losed in quotation marks, owed by speech tags—"he said" "she said"—to indicate the aker. Sometimes speech s can be left out in the logue exchanges, when it lear who is speaking.

TIPS AND TECHNIQUES

When writing dialogue, stick to "he said" or "she said" for your tags most of the time, but use words like "cried" or "whispered" to create some variety or to suit the situation in your story.

USE DRAMATIC DIALOGUE

Subtle information

In Anthony Horowitz's *Stormbreaker*, Alan Blunt tells Alex Rider that they need his help. He explains why:

> *"Have you heard of a man called Herod Sayle?"*
>
> *Alex thought for a moment. "I've seen his name in the newspapers. He's something to do with computers. And he owns racehorses. Doesn't he come from somewhere in Egypt?"*
>
> *"No. Lebanon." Blunt took a sip of wine. "Let me tell you his story, Alex. I'm sure you'll find it of interest. … Herod Sayle was born in complete poverty in the back streets of Beirut."*
>
> Anthony Horowitz, *Stormbreaker*

Blunt then goes on to give the villain's life history. Horowitz needs Alex and the reader to know this information. The rest of the story depends on it. He could have written it as narrative, but then readers might have skimmed it. Instead, to make sure readers take notice, he writes it as part of a conversation. Like Alex, readers "listen" with attention.

Show, don't tell

Dialogue is a very useful storytelling tool. It can carry the story. The Nancy Drew and Hardy Boys stories are told from the omniscient—all-seeing—point of view. Using dialogue avoids having to explain what people are thinking. We simply hear their views in swift, short exchanges, which is very useful in the mystery story genre where there is a lot of deductive reasoning. It would be boring to read about all the characters' thought processes as they solve the mystery. Avoid narrative like this: "Nancy suddenly remembered something. This made her think of another odd incident. She'd not taken much notice of it at the time, but now she began to wonder." How much better to have her exclaim:

> *"Hey, wait a minute, Dad, the witness has to be lying. I've just remembered. George said she saw her downtown. So she couldn't have been at the house when she said she was."*
> Carolyn Keene, *Make No Mistake* (Nancy Drew)

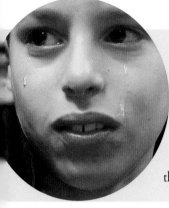

Now it's your turn

Write revealing dialogue

Think about a scene in your story where something quite complicated needs to be explained—some event, or something in a character's history that has made that person act in a certain way. Choose people who are likely to sound different from one another, like an adult and a child. Make them sound angry, disappointed, frightened, or hurt.

Give me a break

Dialogue is used to break up blocks of narrative (storytelling) and give the reader's eyes a rest. It adds variety and pace, too. Good dialogue is quicker to read and conveys information faster than descriptive prose.

Move the story forward

Characters do not make idle chitchat. Whatever they say will convey information—about

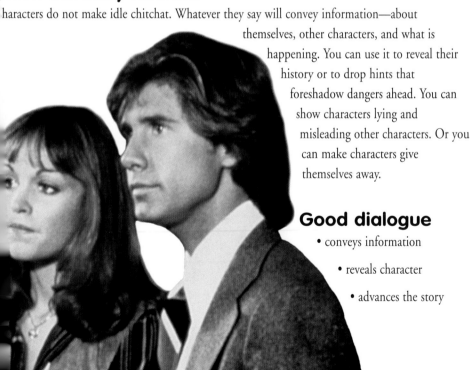

themselves, other characters, and what is happening. You can use it to reveal their history or to drop hints that foreshadow dangers ahead. You can show characters lying and misleading other characters. Or you can make characters give themselves away.

Good dialogue

- conveys information
- reveals character
- advances the story

Let characters sound different from you

Have imaginary conversations with your characters. Try to hear their voices in your head. Here are some varied examples:

AN EDUCATED LAWYER AND A COUNTRY GIRL

Here is Dovey Coe wondering why her lawyer is doing charity work in taking her case. He replies:

"I feel it is part of my job to defend those who can't afford an expensive private attorney. In fact, that is one of the reasons I went into the law. Liberty and justice for all."

"They must pay you a sight of money for you to afford a suit like that."

"No, Miss Dovey," he said, opening his brief-case. "They don't pay me much at all. You certainly speak your mind, don't you?"

Frances O'Roark Dowell, *Dovey Coe*

A VICTORIAN LADY

When Sally Lockhart in *The Ruby in the Smoke* is left an orphan, she is expected to live with an aunt. The aunt quickly lets Sally know what she thinks of the arrangement. She sounds like a cold-hearted but dutiful Victorian English lady:

"I have been told by my lawyer that I am your aunt. I did not expect it; I did not seek it; but I shall not shrink from it." Her voice whined and creaked, thought Sally.

"I have been applying myself with little success to the subject of your future. Do you intend to remain under my care forever, I wonder? Or would five years be sufficient, or ten? I am merely trying to establish the scale of things."

Philip Pullman, *The Ruby in the Smoke*

A teenager in shock

In Joyce Carol Oates' *Big Mouth and Ugly Girl*, Matt is taken by detectives to see the headmaster and accused of trying to blow up his school:

> *Matt's teeth were chattering. He tried to speak calmly.*
> *"Look, this is crazy. I never ... what you're saying?"*
> *"We've had a report, Matt. Two reports. Two witnesses.*
> *They heard you."*
> *"Heard me ... what?"*
> *"Threaten to 'blow up the school.'"*
> *Matt stared at the detective, uncomprehending.*
> *"Threaten to 'massacre' as many people as you could. In the*
> *school cafeteria, just a few hours ago. Are you denying it?"*
> *"Y-yes! I'm denying it."*
> *"You're denying it."*
> *"I think this is all crazy."*
> *"'This is all crazy.' That's your response?"*
>
> Joyce Carol Oates, *Big Mouth & Ugly Girl*

Now it's your turn

A family conversation

Write down a typical conversation between you and your parents. Try to capture exactly how they speak. What words or phrases do they habitually use that are different from yours? Rewrite it with a grandparent or elderly aunt speaking. Now think how your parents speak to their elders. Are there more differences?

TIPS AND TECHNIQUES

Dialogue can reveal differences in age, wealth, and education. Listen to how different people speak. Use what you learn in your fiction.

BEAT WRITER'S BLOCK

When words aren't coming to you, it is called writer's block. If you have been doing plenty of brainstorming exercises, you will already know the antidote to the main cause of writer's block—your internal critic, the real villain.

Destroy the villain

Whenever your internal critic rears up, do a timed brainstorming exercise to fight back. Write something positive about your favorite things or a happy time in your life.

No ideas

There are other causes of writer's block. One is thinking that you have no ideas. But as you have seen previously, ideas are everywhere. The trick is to avoid panicking and to sit quietly and think. Any of the exercises in the book may trigger some creative thoughts.

TIPS AND TECHNIQUES

All stories take their natural time to emerge. If you get stuck with one, start another and go back to the first one later. You won't run out of ideas if you keep reading. But remember: Write your ideas down and keep them together.

Rejection or external criticism

No one enjoys rejection or criticism, but they are important parts of learning to be a writer. If you invite someone to read your stories, you have to prepare yourself for negative comments.

As you develop your writing skills, you will also develop faith in yourself. You will see rejection as a chance to improve your story, if it really needs it.

Grinding to a halt

Another problem is stalling halfway through a story. This can be very discouraging. But when it happens, it is often because you have not thought the story through fully. If it happens to you, try the following exercise—a variation of the one you did on page 33.

Now it's your turn

Kick-start your story

In the middle of a large sheet of paper, draw your hero inside a circle. Imagine that you are that hero. Think about the mystery that you want to solve. Now draw six spokes from your hero circle. Each leads to another circle. Inside each new circle, sketch a different scene or write some notes. Each circle will be a new course of action that you might take or some obstacle that an enemy sets in your path. Give yourself 20 minutes. You may be surprised how your story starts growing.

If you get writer's block that leaves you stuck mid-story, it usually means there has not been enough planning. Maybe some horrible flaw in your plot has cropped up, which might ruin the entire story. Don't panic. There is an answer.

Build character

If a key character (hero or villain) isn't coming to life, do some group brainstorming. Start by writing a brief character description at the top of a sheet of paper. When two minutes are up, ask a friend to add some ideas to yours. Don't worry about writing complete sentences. Thoughts are what count. Keep passing the paper around—the more friends that are willing to join in, the more ideas you will have. Mull over the results. Have you learned something about your character that you didn't know? Do you see him or her in a whole new light?

Compose a group story

Decide among a group of friends what the crime or mystery will be. Then have everyone write a character idea on a piece of paper and drop it into a hat. Each person should pick out a character at random. Then everyone must explain their character and weave him or her into a story. Sit in a circle and take turns explaining each character. Did that character commit the crime? What was the motive? Did he or she have the means and opportunity? There are two rules: Speak your first thoughts, and don't worry if others improve on your ideas. This is not about being clever—it's about shaping a story. The end result will be like a chapter synopsis, which you can develop later, either alone or together. Don't forget the all-important story ingredients—problems, conflict, and resolution.

Now it's your turn

Keep a journal

Write about life at school or home, or record all the details of your hobbies and interests. Set yourself a minimum target length for each entry (such as 300 words). If you use a computer for writing, you can count words easily with the word-count tool. Never write less than your target, even if it means describing the pattern on your bedroom wallpaper or what's in your sandwich. But try to write more. Look for ways to turn the day's events into a story. Did your best friend have a fight with her parents? Write about it.

Photo prompt

Choose an interesting photo from a newspaper. If it's a place, make it the scene of the mystery. If it's a person, make him or her the subject of the mystery. Perhaps he or she has disappeared or been kidnapped. Pass the photo around the group. Everyone has to add their ideas about what has happened. Work out who did it, with what, why, and how.

TIPS AND TECHNIQUES

If all else fails to spark inspiration and break that writer's block, do something completely different. Walk the dog or clean out your bedroom. Doing tasks that give your mind a rest could be just the thing to spring an idea.

TAKE THE NEXT STEP

Finishing your first story, whether it is a short story or a whole novel, is a wonderful achievement. You have searched your imagination and created something entirely new. You have proven you can write, and you have probably learned a lot about yourself, too. Put your story aside for a few weeks, and start a new one.

Another story?

Perhaps while you were writing your first story, an idea started simmering in your mind. Perhaps you made a few notes in your "ideas" file. Do those ideas still excite you? Go back to the start of this book and repeat some of the brainstorming exercises to help you develop the idea further. This time around, you have an advantage. You already know you can write a story.

How about a sequel to your first story?

When thinking about your next work, ask yourself: "Is there more to tell about the characters I have created? Is my hero now hooked on solving mysteries? Can I write a sequel or follow-up story? Is there a minor character whose tale I'm burning to tell?"

Mystery stories lend themselves to series. If you have created an exciting hero, then he or she is bound to want to unravel more mysteries. Readers like series, too. They become intrigued with a particular investigator's methods. Sherlock Holmes, Nancy Drew, the Hardy Boys, Trixie Beldon, Encyclopedia Brown, and the Boxcar Children—they each have a devoted following.

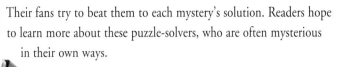

Their fans try to beat them to each mystery's solution. Readers hope to learn more about these puzzle-solvers, who are often mysterious in their own ways.

While you get started on your next whodunnit, remember to keep reading and to study the careers of successful writers. You can learn a lot from people who have mastered this trade.

Think of a title

While your story is "resting," you have a good chance to think of a title. Choosing a snappy story title is another way of hooking your readers. For a mystery book, it's important that the title be intriguing and eye-catching. Think about some titles you know and like, or study the titles on library shelves to get some ideas.

Now it's your turn

No one ever said writing was easy

Write the above sentence at the top of a page. Think about it for a few moments. Then brainstorm for five minutes. Write two lists—all the things you find difficult about writing and all the things you love about it. Now look over your writing problems. Consider them honestly. Are these things that can be fixed with more time, practice, and reading? Is learning to write more important to you than those problems? If the answer is yes, then give yourself a gold star. Your stories will get written.

LEARN FROM THE AUTHORS

You can learn a great deal from hearing how published writers became successful. As you have found from your own experience, no writer would say that writing is easy. Most well-known writers toiled for years before seeing their first stories in print, and few authors earn enough from their books to make a living.

Blue Balliett

Blue Balliett's first novel, the art mystery *Chasing Vermeer*, has been published in 11 languages. Balliett started writing it in 1999, when she was teaching at a Chicago school where the story is set. Her students were writing art mysteries, so she thought she would write one, too. She rewrote her story five times before she was happy with it. She says all the pieces of her life have gone into writing the book.

Anthony Horowitz

Anthony Horowitz, the inventor of the reluctant schoolboy spy Alex Rider, knew he wanted to write from the age of 8, when he asked for a typewriter for his birthday. It was about this time that he was sent away to boarding school, where he had a miserable time and is still getting over it today. He was an overweight, unhappy son of a millionaire father, and he draws on many of his childhood experiences in his writing. He says he's lucky to have two assistant editors at home—his two teenage sons, who have given him lots of advice, including not to use so much description. He listened!

Joan Lowery Nixon

Joan Lowery Nixon (left) wrote more than 140 books during her award-winning career. She was first published at 10 years old—for a poem called "Springtime." She says that for her, a mystery always begins with a question: What would it be like to live in a house where a murder had taken place? How would she feel if a best friend had been arrested for murder? Here are some of her tips for writers:

"Creating suspense in a mystery story is not just a matter of keeping readers guessing. Suspense calls for the emotional responses of anxiety, excitement, and fear."

"Make a list of clues that you can use in your story. One should be the crucial clue … one piece of important information that helps the main character finally solve the mystery."

i Berger Erwin

ki Berger Erwin is the author of the Elizabeth Bryan mystery series, including *The Disappearing* rd *Trick*. She has also written for The Baby-Sitters Club series. Before she starts writing, she ys she has to know:

- the end of her mystery
- why the detective wants to find the solution
- the villain's motive

Then she tries to make the mystery personal. The detective wants to solve the case because it ffects a friend or family member or something else he or she really cares for.

eg Cabot

eg Cabot (right) is the author of The Mediator series and *Princess Diaries*. Her books have become the favorites of y young readers. She says her typical day begins with breakfast a newspaper. Then she gets back into bed, still in her pajamas, writes until 6 or 7 P.M.—unless she has a lunch date. She ys writes on her laptop computer, because her handwriting is : She says, "If you want to be a writer, you have to read! It n't matter what you read, just read as much as possible."

After your story has been resting in your desk for a month, take it out and read through it. You will be able to see your work with fresh eyes and spot flaws more easily.

Edit your work

Reading your work aloud will help you to simplify rambling sentences and correct dialogue that doesn't flow. Cut out all unnecessary adjectives, adverbs, and extra words like "very" and "really." This will instantly make your writing crisper. Once you have cut down the number of words, decide how well the story works. Does it have a satisfying end? Has your hero resolved the conflict in the best possible way? When your story is as good as can be, write it out again or type it up on a computer. This is your manuscript.

Check your title

Is your title interesting? Does it capture your attention and make you want to read the story?

TIPS AND TECHNIQUES

Canadian writer Robert J. Sawyer suggests using the "find" tool in your word-processing program to search for "ly" followed by a space. It will highlight many adverbs you may want to remove. The word "really" will come up, too, and you can usually delete it. Then use this tool to find and delete the word "very." This simple editing will make your text crisper.

professional

u have a computer, you can type up your manuscript and give it a professional look. Manuscripts ld always be printed on one side of white paper, with wide margins and double spacing. Pages ld be numbered, and new chapters should start on a new page. You can also include your title as der on the top of each page. At the front, you should have a title page with your name, address, hone number, and e-mail address.

ake your
n book

ur school has its own computer you could use it to publish own story or to make a story ology (collection) with your ds. A computer will let you se your own font (print style) stify the text (make even-width gins like a professionally printed). When you have typed and d your story to a file, you can it quickly with the spell check

grammar check. You might want to move sections of your story around using the cut-and-paste , which saves a lot of rewriting. Having your story on a computer file also means you can print a whenever you need one. Or you can revise the whole , if you want.

sign a cover

e your story is in good shape, print it out. Then use computer to design the cover. A graphics program will ou scan and print your own artwork or download y-made graphics. You could also use your own digital ographs and learn how to manipulate them on the puter screen to produce some original images. Try g yourself or your friends as models for your story's es or villains.

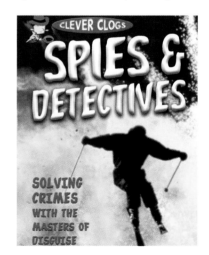

CLEVER CLOGS
SPIES &
DETECTIVES
SOLVING CRIMES WITH THE MASTERS OF DISGUISE

The next step is to find an audience for your mystery story. Family members or classmates may be receptive. Or you may want to share your work through a magazine a publishing house, or a Web site.

Some places to publish your story

There are several magazines and a number of writing Web sites that accept stories and novel chapters from young mystery writers. Some also give writing advice. Several run regular competitions. Each site has its own rules about submitting work, so make sure you read them carefully before you send in a story. Here are some more ideas:

• Send stories to your school newspaper. If your school doesn't have a newspaper, start your own with like-minded friends.

• Keep your eyes peeled when reading your local newspaper or magazines. They might be running writing competitions you could enter.

• Check with local museums and colleges. Some run creative-writing workshops during school holidays.

Writing clubs

Starting a writing club or workshop is a great way to get your mystery story out there. Exchanging stories will also get you used to criticism from others, which will be very useful in learning how to write. Your local library might be kind enough to provide a space for such a club.

Finding a publisher

If you decide to send your manuscript to a publisher, secure it with a staple or a paper clip. Always enclose a short letter (explain what you are sending) and a stamped, self-addressed envelope for the story's return. Study the market, and find out which publishers are most likely to publish mystery fiction. Addresses of publishers and information about whether they accept submissions can be found in writers' handbooks. Bear in mind that manuscripts that haven't been asked for or paid for by a publisher—unsolicited submissions—are rarely published.

Writer's tip

If your story is rejected by an editor, see it as a chance to make it better. Try again. Remember that having your work published is wonderful, but it is not the only thing. Being able to make up a story is a gift, so why not give yours to someone you love? Read it to a younger brother or sister. Tell it to your grandmother. Find your audience.

Case study

When award-winning author Avi was in school, nobody thought he was very smart. He wanted to prove to people that he could be a good writer, and he worked hard at it. It took years before he had a book published. But now he says, "Don't assume that because everyone believes a thing it is right or wrong."

Some final words

Through stories, we can explore all the good and bad things that make us human. This is what storytelling is about. It gives us hope. It shows us new possibilities. It sends us chasing endless curiosities and allows us to see what else we can discover and learn.

Read! Write!

And keep looking for those mysteries.

CHAPTER 10: FIND OUT MORE

GLOSSARY

back story—the history of characters and events that happened before the story begins

chapter synopsis—an outline that describes briefly what happens in each chapter

cliffhanger—ending a chapter or scene of a story at a nail-biting moment

dramatic irony—when the reader knows something the characters don't

editing—removing all unnecessary words from your story, correcting errors, and rewriting the text until the story is the best it can be

editor—the person at a publishing house who finds new books to publish and advises authors on how to improve their stories by telling them what needs to be added or cut

first-person viewpoint—a viewpoint that allows a single character to tell the story as if he or she had written it; readers feel as if that character is talking directly to them; for example: "It was July when I left for Timbuktu. Just the thought of going back there made my heart sing."

foreshadowing—dropping hints of coming events or dangers that are essential to the outcome of the story

genre—a particular type of fiction, such as fantasy, historical, adventure, mystery, science, or realistic

manuscript—your story when it is written down, either typed or by hand

metaphor—calling a man "a mouse" is a metaphor, a word picture; from it we learn in one word that the man is timid or weak, not that he is actually a mouse

motivation—the reason why a character does something

narrative—the telling of a story

omniscient viewpoint—an all-seeing narrator that sees all the characters and tells readers how they are acting and feeling

plot—the sequence of events that drives a story forward; the problems that the hero must resolve

point of view (POV)—the eyes through which a story is told

lisher—a person or company who pays for an author's manuscript to be
ted as a book and who distributes and sells that book

uel—a story that carries an existing one forward

ile—saying something is like something else, a word picture, such as "clouds like
ed lace"

opsis—a short summary that describes what a story is about and introduces the
n characters

me—the main issue that the story addresses, such as good versus evil, how power
corrupts, the importance of truth, and so on; a story
can have more than one theme

third-person viewpoint—a viewpoint
that describes the events of a story
through a single character's
eyes, such as "Jem's heart
leapt in his throat. He'd
been dreading this
moment for months."

unsolicited submission—
a manuscript that is sent
to a publisher without
being requested; these
submissions usually end
up in the "slush pile,"
where they may wait a long
time to be read

writer's block—when writers
think they can no longer write or
have used up all their ideas

Further information

Visit your local libraries and make friends with the librarians. They can direct you to useful sources of information, including magazines that publish young people's short fiction. You can learn your craft and re great stories at the same time. Librarians will also know if any published authors are scheduled to speak in your area.

Many authors visit schools and offer writing workshops. Ask your teacher to invite a favorite author to spea at your school.

On the Web

For more information on this topic, use FactHound.
1. Go to *www.facthound.com*
2. Type in this book ID: 0756516412
3. Click on the *Fetch It* button.
FactHound will find the best Web sites for you.

Read more mysteries

Blacker, Terence. *The Angel Factory*. New York: Simon & Schuster Books for Young Readers, 2002.

Campbell, Julie. *The Secret of the Mansion*, Trixie Belden series. New York: Random House, 2003.

Corder, Zizou. *Lionboy*. New York: Dial Books, 2004.

Cross, Gillian. *Wolf*. New York: Holiday House, 1991.

DeFelice, Cynthia. *The Ghost of Fossil Glen*. New York: Farrar, Straus and Giroux, 1998.

Dowell, Frances O'Roark. *Dovey Coe*. New York: Atheneum Books for Young Readers, 2000.

Fitzgerald, John D. *The Great Brain Is Back*. New York: Dial Books for Young Readers, 1995.

Garfield, Leon. *The Empty Sleeve*. New York: Delacorte Press, 1988.

Horowitz, Anthony. *Stormbreaker*. New York: Philomel Books, 2001.

Lawrence, Caroline. *The Enemies of Jupiter (T Roman Mysteries)*. New Milford, Conn.: Roari Brook Press, 2005.

Nixon, Joan Lowery. *The Kidnapping of Christi Lattimore*. Orlando, Fla.: Harcourt, 2004.

Peck, Richard. *The Ghost Belonged to Me*. San Barbara, Calif.: Cornerstone Books, 1989.

Roberts, Willo Davis. *The View from the Cher Tree*. New York: Atheneum Books for Young Readers, 1998.

Stolz, Mary. *Casebook of a Private (Cat's) Eye*. Chicago: Front Street/Cricket Books, 1999.

Read all the Write Your Own books:

Write Your Own Adventure Story
ISBN: 0-7565-1638-2

Write Your Own Fantasy Story
ISBN: 0-7565-1639-0

Write Your Own Historical Fiction Story
ISBN: 0-7565-1640-4

Write Your Own Mystery Story
ISBN: 0-7565-1641-2

Write Your Own Realistic Fiction Story
ISBN: 0-7565-1642-0

Write Your Own Science Fiction Story
ISBN: 0-7565-1643-9

Picture Credits: Alamy: 24 all, 25 all, 38 all, 46 all. Cadmium: 4-5 all, 6-7 all, 10 all, 11b, 13 al 17t, 18-19 all, 45t, 47r, 48-49 all, 50-51 all, 52b, 53b, 54t, 56 all, 57t. Corbis RF: 8b, 8-9c, 16l 27 all, 28-29 all, 32-33 all, 34-35 all, 36 all, 44t, 54b, 55 all. Creatas: 12 all, 20-21 all, 30t, 30-3 39c, 40-41 all, 42 all, 52t, 58-59 all, 61c. FBI: 16b. Rex Features: 1, 8t, 9t, 10-11c, 14-15c, 17c 22-23 all, 26t, 26-27c, 37t, 39b, 43b, 44-45b, 53t. Every effort has been made to contact copyri holders of any material reproduced in this book. Any omissions will be rectified in subsequent printings if notice is given to the publishers.